This book belongs to:

____

22431536R00066

Printed in Great Britain
by Amazon